MAPPING THE MAZE

To Pat and Ken

with love

[signature]

x

OTHER PUBLICATIONS

MAPPING THE MAZE

ALISON CHISHOLM

HEADLAND

First published in 2004
by
HEADLAND PUBLICATIONS
38 York Avenue, West Kirby,
Wirral CH48 3JF

British Library Cataloguing in Publication Data
A full CIP record for this book is available
from the British Library

ISBN 1 902096 85 1

Printed in Great Britain by
L. Cocker & Co., Berry Street, Liverpool L1 4JQ

HEADLAND acknowledges the financial
assistance of Arts Council England

for **Brenda, Donna, Mike and Ted**

ACKNOWLEDGEMENTS

Some of these poems have appeared in *Acumen*, *Cross and Screen, Envoi, Murhill Poems, No Choice but to Trust, Orbis, Parents, Perceptions, Poets' England: Derbyshire, Poetry Monthly, Poetry Nottingham International, STAR TREK the poems, The Woman Writer, Waiting for You to Speak* and *Writers' Forum,* or have been broadcast by BBC Radio Merseyside and BBC Radio North West.

'Through a Lens Darkly' won the Wells Literature Festival 2001 International Poetry Competition. 'Pearls' won the 2002 Sefton Poetry Competition.

CONTENTS

WEIGHT OF WORDS

FIRE CHILD

EARTH AND AIR

GOODIES AND BADDIES

WET WET WET

WRITE PLACES

KINDS OF LOVING

HOME AND AWAY

SITUATION VACANT

A vacancy has arisen
for an experienced poem,
well versed, articulate,
equally qualified in truth and beauty.

The successful applicant
will possess profound communication skills,
and be typed single spaced
on one side of the paper only.

It shall have a working knowledge
of iambic pentameter, and be willing to undertake
advanced courses in dactyl and trochee management.

Duties will consist of arranging
the best words in the best order,
whispering through stillness,
and making sense of the universe.
A little light alliteration may also be required.

Payment is modest,
but accommodation between hard covers
will be provided.

Fringe benefits include
editorial feedback, spell checks -
and guaranteed immortality
for the right candidate.

NEW START

Midnight. At the year's turn
we stood outside, drawn by a sense
of wonder, rebirthing. Girls in silk,
dark suited men, warm of wine
and dinner, we carried flutes of bubbles,
raised our glasses to the moon.

It was a time of kissing, crisp
as January, inched by second hand,
settled in first snowflakes. Air
was charged; anticipation burst
in fireworks, scarlet, green stars
cascading, silver rain and indigo.

And I recalled one phrase -
new start - a mantra to be chanted
in the mind, while open voice
called greetings to neighbours, passers by.
We stood an hour, each tick,
each heartbeat thrilling ... new start, new start.

Day could not break the spell. We walked
beside the water, we and half the town,
still wishing strangers happiness,
still rapt in atmosphere
no other day could generate
within the whisper of our lifetime.

Pacing beyond those days, we talk
of good intentions, tiny promises and vast.
There are no broken resolutions, just
the offer of new start, new start
if we should slip; and as we move
the party and the world fall into step.

CHOOSING WORDS

Tyres champ tarmac, gorge an hour.
Along the route I plan the things I'll say.
I'll mention the mild weather,
ask about her job, and has she chosen curtains?

I'll leave unsaid
questions of money,
boyfriends, and the new directions
which signpost distances away from me.

Last miles seem slowest,
inch the journey on,
scatter my intentions.
Greetings give way
to unwise words. Intrusive, loaded,
they weigh between us,
define our differences,
pull in opposite ways.

CLOSE ENCOUNTER

CAPTAIN'S LOG ...

For days now we have been orbiting
a cloud of unidentified matter.
The crew are baffled; computer cannot probe
the mass of data stored within.
We have put up our shields
and engaged maximum warp -
but we cannot escape the tractor beam
that drags us back.

From its interior the cloud exudes
a kind of music. All who recognise it
make report of different frequencies, as if
each hears a song unique to each,
sways to a unique rhythm.

Even the Betazoid cannot decipher
nuances of meaning issuing
from the cloud's depths. Only
when its mists thin, she reads a hint
of its message - enough to know
it is trying to communicate.

The delay is causing problems. We are aiming
to get back on course - and yet
my officers are finding it difficult to concentrate,
obsessed with learning all the cloud.

CAPTAIN'S LOG SUPPLEMENTAL ...

The whole ship's company is now engaged
in analysing the amorphous mass. At least
we have a designation for it now.
It's called a poem.

PICTURE THIS

First, prime your canvas. Let your mind
lose shopping lists and business meetings.
Give it moths and sunsets,
the feel of earth through fingers.

Flood nouns and verbs onto your empty palette;
mix with hint of adjective, shade of pronoun;
fill your brush.

Skim words to break the whiteness,
imagination blending cockatoo and coffee;
tennis, tickling and trains.

Bristles define each separate strand,
divide phrases, punctuate.

Watch images emerge as brush and knife
paint seaside shouts, sleet to spatter skin,
taste of buttered corn, the vastness
of an atom.

Animate with metred pulsebeats, making lines
leap in the foreground, sweep
to give perspective.

Stipple rhymes, rebounding sound on sound,
teasing reflections
where sky touches land.

And when rhythm, shadow,
texture, stanza meet,
fill mind and retina,
inform, inspire,

then reach out,
select another canvas
broader, wider than you ever dreamed

and start again.

FIRE CHILD

My Leo birth was ordered by the sun,
and I am drawn by amber, orange, gold.
Fire seeking, brash kaleidoscopes of fun
stand, yell their message, overblown and bold.
So yellow fantasies run uncontrolled
in dreams of marmalade and tangerine.
November leaves and ripened peaches hold
unseasoned memories, whose pastel green
soon passed and faded. In a gilded sheen
fire opals dance and sparkle, embers glow
through last warm rays, and on a blazing screen
pyre bright and fierce, the blaring sun sets low.
No fading hints of shadow could destroy
the radiant Fire Child's aura, rich with joy.

HOARDER

I am a hoarder of names,
collector of identities. I have learned
where this man worked, that woman lived
a hundred years ago; and earlier, I know the parishes
where fusions of DNA began my countdown.

I am a hoarder of images,
sketches and photographs. I see
curve of my smile, lift of an eyebrow
twisted from true in time's
distorted mirror.

I am a hoarder of cells,
holding molecules close
in my skin, in my blood,
a living testament of other lives
who gave me mine.

JACKS

Ten silver, six-point stars, a rubber ball,
were everything my universe required.
With twist of hand I tried to snatch for all
ten silver, six-point stars. A rubber ball
bounced steady thuds till Mother's nerves were raw -
I played for hour on hour and never tired.
Ten silver, six-point stars, a rubber ball -
were everything my universe required.

SELECTIVE EDUCATION

Special Offer! Free for all
for a full twelve years or more.

Go to school. Assimilate
reading, writing, geography,

the massed knowledge
of every culture on earth.

Learn cricket, typing, everything
you don't need to know about sex.

Okay. So how is it I can buy stamps
in six languages, and can't wire a plug?

MEMORIES

I remember ranks of green-cased Miners lipsticks,
orange glow of foundation, black eyeliner,
white nails, 'The Palest' palest lips.

I remember Saturday nights
of mushroom vol-au-vents, 'Batman'
and 'Hey hey, we're the Monkees,'
blue Rimmel eye shadow, op-art brooch.

I remember the youth club,
dancing to 'She Loves You' in the church hall,
his cotton shirt, silk cravat
and holding hands warm all the way home.

I remember Radio Caroline,
snogging in the cinema, coke and crisps
in the bandstand on wet Saturdays,
tennis club Sundays.

I remember how I felt the day
they sent his unit to Ulster.

WAITING IN THE WINGS

Dry-mouthed, I wait backstage,
heart thumping, script forgotten,
hearing from a distance words
that draw me closer. I cannot remember
my part in the play,
the reason for this costume.
The cue propels me centre stage,
puts lines between my lips,
and these in turn
force movement, make me hide
so my character can come alive.

By the final curtain I am there,
not merely confident
but whole. Applause
is taken as my due.

Dry-mouthed, I watch backstage,
as others leave in jeans and sweatshirts -
look down at my costume, these strange robes.
I know that I must kill
the character who wears them,
turn into myself,
live beyond the stage;
but something's different.
I stand. Root.
Wait in the wings.

GINGERBREAD

I have stopped walking the forest,
following fox routes and rabbit ways.
I do not need
to hold my brother's hand.

I no longer dream
of woodcutters striding out of cottage doors,
the gleam of axe
as they turn away.

I am not obsessed
with pushing old women into ovens,
back tracking paths
to find my way home.

But sometimes, all I want
is to fill my mouth with gingerbread,
let its warm spice burn my throat,
let rich crumbs conjure risk.

ISLAND TALES

I am lying on soft sand
dressed in sunlight,
drunk on air that breathes spiced rum.

I am silent, still,
doing nothing, thinking nothing,
letting earth's rotation slow
to my tempo. My tune
is heart's rhythm; my voice
the tern's cry.

I am coconut and mango,
salt and surf. An island girl,
I fill your mind with stories -
tempt you to believe.

CHRISTMAS DAY

1 am: The waiting ends. We walk home,
frost tanging our cheeks,
to mulled wine, mince pies, poetry.

4 am: I start awake, hear echo
of muffled giggles, "Has he been?"
paper and ribbons ripping.
Christmas past fades. The present
is rattled catflap, hailstones on glass.

7.30: The Teasmade carols. Fragmented videos
taunt my mind's screen. I reach for the remote.
Disney is safer. Together
we learn love in packages,
smart as we note omissions.

10 am: "Yea, Lord, we greet Thee" and five candles
indicate another year's full circle.

12.30: Absent friends assume a darker shape.
I swallow fast, let bubbles
scour my gullet; then pick up the ginger cat,
hide behind his hissing protestations.
The turkey beckons, beguiles
with chestnut and cranberries.

3 pm: Articulating ritual messages,
the queen competes with syncopated snoring;
loses. Even the youngest droops,
eyes shut, still fingering
his new toy fire engine.

6 pm: Nobody wants to eat. We butter rolls,
add turkey slices, ham or cheese.
Every crumb vanishes.

7.30: The children coax us to play games,
bring Jenga and jigsaws, urge charades.
We join in to amuse them; fail to notice
when they creep off to the computer.

11 pm: You mix the final G and T. I try to guess
how many calories in a peanut;
give up; salt my palm with a dozen.

1 am: We lie close, arms entwined,
breathing the same air.
Another line of shingle sets its memory.
The tinsel tide is ebbing.

LIVING HISTORY

Fifties baby, sixties child, for me
'the war' was far away. I learned
from history classes, TV comedies;
could not imagine Mum and Dad involved.

Dad spoke little of those days;
would answer questions - offered nothing more.
Snapshots of young men smiled from beaches,
and wedding photos featured uniforms.

Mum made me laugh with tales of how,
in blitzed December, all the Christmas store
of rationed food, collected over weeks,
was eaten when they thought
they'd not see morning: how the neighbours
pooled their share of eggs and sugar, fruit,
to make her wedding cake.

Nineties orphan, I learned truths
from papers found too late for asking: an account
of one young airman's hours
in Arctic Circle waters -
and my ration book.

BROTHER

Sometimes I wonder
what you would have looked like -
taller than me
but still blue eyed and pale?

Would you have understood
The Flowerpot Men
and atomic numbers?
Played football
or shared my books?

Just too young for National Service,
would you have liked
to play with cap-guns,
shoot Red Indians, pluck the legs
from a crane fly?

Would you have listened to Cliff or Elvis?
Beatles or Stones?
Worn blue jeans or leathers?

And if you were not miscarried,
where would I be?

Would I be?

SEA STORIES

I swim,
my body's pressure bruising sea
already pitted, mirror to the crags
that soar, shadowless.
Water whispers ebb and flow secrets,
tells of boats and fish,
of net and wrack,
of tidal surges when the earth heaves.

I slow crawl to a rock
beyond the bay's curve,
clamber out. It absorbs
unsalted water, sucks a dark stain,
holds fragments of my being here
locked in time's memory.

Tales of brine and boulder
cry on gull's wing, grow in coral.

Stirring a rock pool with my toe
startles a crab, whose sideways dart
pulls rays of sun to strike
new angles. Their energy
pulsates to rhythms gathered through the void
of star and quicksilver.

I slither back into the waves,
know breakers and spume
that shock to my presence,
hear mermaids' stories,
insistent song of sirens.

And I am myth, becoming part
of noon's completeness,
melting as each cell reacts
with water, cliffs, and gulls, and sun.

GUT FEELING

This is not your element.
Breathe evenly. Make panic's tide
break in harmless ripples.
Put your face in the water. Open your eyes.
Do not forget to breathe.

> Alien seas invade, relentless,
> and skin cannot resist.
> You feel exponential growth inside.

Look down. Concentrate
until fog of swirled sand
settles grains, regroups
to shimmer a fish.
Do not forget to breathe.

> Blood pressure is checked,
> your pulse rate monitored,
> fluid drawn from the shifting mass.

Pinch your nose and swallow.
Again. All's well. Swim deeper,
where jade weed darkens,
sun's light is eclipsed.
Do not forget to breathe.

> Your fingers' searching
> meets resistance. Aspirate.
> Then hold your breath to stay all movement.

Let weights pull you further,
thrusting whelk and cockle shells
to bruise your palms. Kick
against the drift. Suck and swallow.
Do not forget to breathe.

SEVEN FACES

I am mother, my body the power house
constructing, nurturing, nourishing,
pushing my perfect creation into spluttering life.
I take rich beef, wash, cube, seal and sear.

I am manager, balancing accounts,
deciding when to buy cars or coffee,
knowing what time to leave for school,
a breathing diary of appointments with dentist and teacher.
I peel carrots, paring orange ribbons, chop into hexagonal discs.

I am lover, soft whisperinng,
making every touch a caress, my ardour brimming,
ready to be ignited by his kiss,
incandescent in his arms.
I rip at onions' parchment, find the shimmering globe.

I am independent, working, earning,
light years from my kitchen
where colleagues do not know my other lives.
I strip garlic, pound its pungent clove.

I am homemaker, singing as I scrub red tiles,
spraying polish, catching up the dust. Rhythms
- of sweeping, washing, wiping - keep time
with inspirations of the bricks and timber,
shudderings as they exhale.
I thicken juices, sauce the casserole.

I am mediator, negotiating noise levels
with neighbours, adjudicating bathtime squabbles.
I sprinkle salt, watch as it permeates.

I am artist, making quilted images
to fix in memory, stories of princess and dragon,
music so that each can dance to an individual tune.
I pour red wine, steep the meat in its bouquet.

I am me. I celebrate;
smile as I serve.

PARTIAL RECALL

From forty or so years away, there is a blur
in memories of childhood, soft focussing
on spade-and-bucket holidays, birthday teas,
the shops for shoes and dresses,
sequences of assemblies, lessons, homework.

A day, a week ago there is a blur
of teaching, cleaning, writing,
deciding to have .... something for dinner.
I cannot recall clothes I chose to wear,
people I met, jokes or conversations.

Yet seventy-eight-and-one-third months ago
I sat in a charcoal plastic chair,
(my back to the window and November night,)
garish in shocking pink sweat suit, wearing
Chanel Number Five and the ruby ring he helped me
    choose,

and holding my father's hand
as the numbers on the screen slipped
ninety - eighty-eight - eighty-five - seventy-two
and a single tear ran from the inner corner of his closed
    eye,
mapping its moist route down his cheek.

JUNE 17th 2000
For the Centenary of Nana's Birth

Today I can feel breath
cool on my neck when no one's there.
I see dusk sky veined with gold
and dark reliefs of tree,
silhouettes more solid
at night; know your fingers
wind their branches.

Today I can count
each separate pair of chromosomes,
apportion some to you.

And once again I am kneeling
before the chair, book propped
on brown velvet cushions,
coca cola and sherbet dabs nearby.
I discover spells
concealed in poetry's magic,
superheroes in mild mannered disguise,
the gold on claret leather
cloaking Shakespeare.

Today I sense your touch
bringing me to life.

Today, as azure edges purple,
I shut the door on your century,
move forward
clutching close your gifts.

WOMEN'S WARD

Four beds squat, one in each corner,
and there are flowers on every shelf and table,
bowl bright and flooding vases,
for we are women, sick with women's things,
and flowers articulate the words men cannot.

Four of Eve's faces smudge the pillows -
nervous young mother, aging whore, nice wife,
and ... me. I observe, ignore the baby babble,
innuendo, chat. My words are clustering
in hidden places, dividing, multiplying.

Sharing pain, we ape each other's funny walks,
discover agony of climbing in a bath.
Nurses, intimate as sponge and towel,
tell only jokes that make us smile,
know belly laughs would burst our stitches.

Dynamics change when visitors arrive.
No longer sisters, each becomes
the hub to satellites of partners, children, friends.
Our common language has no meaning,
and we re-learn four separate idioms.

Flowers begin to droop; and rounds
of pulses, pain and pills and cups of tea
count down towards the day we leave.
We thank the doctors, say we'll keep in touch
with one another, don't mean it.

Four beds are sheeted, new names fixed,
before we go. And we take home
a lightened burden, strands
of camaraderie to loose in convalescence.

But when memory's surface
sloughs those seven days,
my rooted thoughts spread tentacles
bearing traces of four women's essence
that fix themselves in deepest caverns,
that will not disappear.

RESONANCE

Do not inter my bones when I am gone.
Instead, when flesh dissolves, let music start
in rhythm with the pulse of my dead heart.
Use phalanges as sticks to tap upon
the drum that was my skull. Where eyes once shone
fix cymbals in their socket. Wrench apart
my vertebrae for ocarinas, chart
your staves on shins, make ribs your xylophone.

I need you to remember, know me by
a presence, resonating down the years,
that stirs the air with music made of me.
If I am music, I can never die,
can never be destroyed; so mortal fears
dissolve, and I have immortality.

PERSPECTIVE

The world is upside down.
Clouds have solidified -
slabbed into white squares;
a mailbox hangs in air,
breeze touched, and beside it
a mint-green lobster threatens.

I walk at a new angle,
surprised by lemon skies,
the vivid blue of rocks and grass.

I cannot remember
if these changes happened suddenly
or over years. Dreams
assume the pattern of my old days,
where road and house
never shifted, rain was wet.

Looking-glass logic
informs my retina. I know
I should look beyond,
regain perspective.

Instead I play hopscotch on the clouds,
pluck purple grass,
dodge the lobster's claws.

SWAN FLIGHT

Viewed from a train,
two swans etch lines beneath the clouds,
charcoal against a monochrome sky,
necks extended, massive wings
spread to catch the wind's thrust.

The brand of their image
cameos a day of cabs stuck in traffic,
meetings, sandwich lunch.

They animate the journey home,
inspire the stuffy carriage,
lend smooth speed when tracks
are overleaved.

Restrained by timetable and second hand
in days that follow
thoughts are minuted;
but misted hours recall
a glimpse of pewter, window framed -
a streak of swan.

PAPERWEIGHT CINQUAIN

Glazed, fixed,
trapped in bubbles
air molecules jostle,
cry freedom, know infinity
beckons.

UNDERWORLD

Cave black is total dark.
You stand, weightless, bearing
the weight of the world above you;
and hear at earth's heart
shift and settle of rock,
roaring of the molten core.

You are alone, so alone
since you squeezed through that fissure
leaving light and measured hours behind.
You reach to touch
the cavern walls, find nothing
but air, heavy with grit.

You are dizzy with the spin
of earth, numbed by its pressure,
your presence counted out in heartbeats;
yet you are the dot
fuelling motion,
the planet's pivot.

Pain barbs the struggle back
to light and gravity.
Familiar air snatches cold,
ages in your lungs. Grasp
memory's blanket tight before
you fall back, grounded.

MISTLETOE

Missel spread, apple nurtured,
pearls nestle in their sickle of green,
each bead promising kisses.

These sprigs express pale pledges -
all-heal to ease pain,
a charm to ward off witches.

Fable's weight endows mixed messages:
Aeneas' Golden Bough was plucked
from oak beside hell's gate,
and Baldur's fatal wound
was arrowed in mistletoe; yet sprays
protect from evil, keep babies safe.

Christmas cut, the garland's pallor warms
with candle light. It hangs in twilit air,
never touching earth, gleaming
moon beams of hope
for all who linger in its shadow.

Peace resides where berries flourish,
welcoming at village inn or cottage;

but the priest shrinks from pagan ties,
sees druids' golden shears
reflected in their sheen,
hears a white bull bellow.

STONE HAIKUS

Hold the stone tightly.
Feel smoothness, years and healing
revitalising.

Pink and grey mingle,
form new colour, new texture,
defy rock-bound rules.

When I touch this stone
I know all the world's answers -
most of its questions.

CLICHÉ

They came between dusk blue
and the watery moon's rising,
arrows of geese
that made the sky a river
flecked with froth.

Their calling silvered the air,
reflected in glass and puddles,
made twilight a cliché.

But one small boy
who knew geese only from a picture book
watched,
gasped,
wondered.

LOW DOWN

I do not run well, lumbering, wobbling ...
from a standing start
I could scarcely crest the meadow grass.
The cat's call spurs me.
Those silver horns are not
much larger than my own. So all
that's needed is an extra kick ...

and now the laughing, the laughing,
and my dishes are fading into dim distance,
and all my spoons cascading out of sight.

KEY

I enter hidden chambers,
force locks to tumble,
open the way.

I am anonymous
in pocket or purse,
find my identity
at consummation.

I know oil,
am bright metal,
turn easily.

Guard me with care.
I know your secrets;
I collaborate.

BEWARE HANDSOME PRINCES

He will offer you love
in an ivory tower,
doves to take grain
from your fingers,
nightingales to trill your dreams.

He will offer you castles,
solid structures
with walls to protect,
that will strut his power
before his enemies.

He will offer you gold,
fine silks, amethysts
and sapphires reflecting your eyes,
and make manacles
of diamond rings.

Remember, a portcullis
will keep you safe
but make the tower a prison;
and arrow slits are not wide enough
for blowing kisses through.

ONCE MORE WITH FEELING

Roll up! Roll up!
See the russet acrobat
turn somersaults,
undulate across the grass.
Gasp as he scales the bird table
to sneak a peanut,
spirals down its stand.
Laugh when the robin buzzes him,
scares him into leaping at an oak,
skimming its bark.
Applaud his bow, fanned tail flourished,
eyes alert for titbits.

Move inside past banks
of floral tributes, Father's Day cards,
regimented, brass vased chrysanthemums,
olive velvet curtains.

He waits in his tiring house
under the hydrangea.
Another hearse approaches,
another queue in black and navy.

Roll up! Roll up!
Another performance. Another exit.

DOUBLE JEOPARDY

You ask me how I know that I can kill?
The answer lies in words you never spoke.
If I can't have you, dear, then no-one will.

You led me on, and with magician's skill
you conjured promises you promptly broke.
You ask me how I know that I can kill;

determination steeled my heart until
I longed to squeeze your neck, to hear you choke.
If I can't have you, dear, then no-one will.

You toyed with me, your laughter harsh and shrill.
To break my heart was just your little joke.
You ask me how I know that I can kill?

And when your bluff was called, and when you still
refused me, mentioned him just to provoke ....
If I can't have you, dear, then no-one will

enjoy the favours you're so keen to spill,
aroused by all the passions you evoke.
You ask me how I know that I can kill.
If I can't have you, dear, then no-one will.

HANDS

Mesmerised by your hands,
I see your fingers, squat, ingrained
with good earth, holding spade or scythe.
The woman weeps,
tells how they brushed her throat.

At my table, you held a knife and fork,
made intricate passes cutting food;
used those same hands to rend her clothes,
tie her stocking at her neck,
bruise her arms, her breasts.

You folded paper boats, laughed
as you helped my niece to float them.
Now I learn those fingertips clawed flesh,
forced a knife at her gut, slit skin.

I chided like a mother
when you bit your nails. I hear
how they raked her thighs, drew blood.

She heaves as she describes your hands
wrenching her legs apart. I close my eyes -
still see your palms extended,
try not to look at the junction
where your life line crossed mine.

GREEN MAN

He lives in line of leaf vein,
lichen stains,
moss that sponges stone.

He urges bud and blossom,
hears blackbird's call and thrush's,
watches vole and rabbit.

He weeps at trodden grass,
bleeds when branches break,
cools in spread of fern.

His breath animates,
greens the forest;
reincarnates.

BAANANA

From half a mile away
the yellow splodge of you cheers.
You spill sunshine on the tarmac.

Closer, and your tail's clown grin
widens and welcomes, stretches
the biggest smile in Liverpool.

Facing you, I am overwhelmed
by the soft suggestion of your ears,
vulnerable tilt of your head.

I press my hands against your flank.
Rough gold resists. You
are irresistible. I laugh out loud.

ORLANDO

I sing the cat, the ginger stripes and gold
in fur as satin soft as thistledown.
Full grown but kitten sized, his tiny weight
can warm your lap, monopolise your couch.

I sing the cat, whose mewing call demands
immediate attention - fish or cream,
or, stranger, melon juice or monkeynuts,
or toffee yoghurt shared at breakfast time.

I sing the cat whose curiosity
takes him through other people's catflaps, lures
him into cars, to gardens streets away,
or settles him on neighbours' chairs or beds.

I sing the cat who lies in ambush, springs,
attacks our tabby, romps and chases her;
then frolics in the garden catching worms
so gently I can set them free unhurt.

I sing the cat whose purr of deep content
can soothe away the troubles of the day,
who breathes warm life into the coldest room,
and holds my heart in fragile, furry paws.

CAROL SINGING

Pity the poor old carollers
When December's bitter and drear,
And icicles drop from the top of the roof
To freeze off their Christmas cheer.
Their mittens are dripping and soggy,
And their boots let in the snow.
They may ask How Far to Bethlehem?
But the public don't want to know.

Pity the poor old carollers
As the rain begins to fall
And they have to Ding Dong Merrily
At the thought of the babe in the stall.
The snow is churning to muddy slush,
And nobody's feeling jolly,
But they have to drone on about Decking the Halls
With bough after bough of holly.

Pity the poor old carollers
As they plod from street to street
With ears that sting and noses that run
And no feeling left in their feet.
A sense of duty makes them sing
Of Royal David's City,
But unlike the shepherds watching their flocks,
They are hardly sitting pretty.

Pity the pool old carollers
As the hour grows late; and night
Turns icier, blacker and bleaker still
And the last port of call's out of sight.
And who can blame them for giving up
On the coldest night of the year,
For hushing the Herald Angels to make
Their next stop the next bar for a beer?

SERIAL CALLER

January slouches in shadows,
shrugs into his trenchcoat, pulls down his hat,
darkens afternoons.

He spits contempt -
sleet that rattles on your windows,
rain battering the porch.

Ragged on park bench and pavement
he coughs a fog
of 'flu, hawks pneumonia.

When he sleeps
the moon ices night, frosts
grimy scraps of newspaper gusted in corners.

He's a stayer:
slugs it out to the last day,
grips February's coat tails, holds fast.

His grumbling still echoes
when March shakes out winter's sheets.
You just know he'll be back.

WRECK OF THE DEMETER, WHITBY 18-

Rusted water boils dark with blood, not wine,
whipped by storm strong enough
to smash 'Demeter.' The harbour
is livid with sunset, red-lighting sailors home.

With one wolf-bound he clears the wreck.
Streets narrow as coffins try to lure him.
Taverns are brash, ale-stale;
their brightness repels.

Stone steps lead high to Abbey ruins.
He flinches; slinks in shadows;
shies away from the Celtic cross
at heaven's staging post.

Drawn by the stench of rotting fish
he prowls the quay; late gulls circle,
wail as they scavenge, swooping
to claim discarded guts and scale.

Wavelets lap slap fishing boats,
froth frilling their edges.
He sees beyond to deeper water
brimstone bubbling,

longs for black, chill silence
of his element, a tomb
for undead habitation, time-whiling
till his blood lust stalks again.

LESSON

They taunted him, and mocked him for a fool;
he let resentment simmer, fester, grow.
Who would have thought his 'friends' could be so cruel?
And which of those tormenting youths could know
the scheme he nurtured; take a gun to school,
defeat the bullies with a single blow?

Each jibe held power to bruise, a body blow
for one who knew that he was not a fool
in spite of all their jeering. There was no
escape for him from vicious tongues and cruel
abuse. He knew he must ignore, or grow
a thicker skin to carry him through school.

Nobody listened. No one in the school
could shield him from his suffering, or blow
the wicked words away. He played the fool,
a desperate act, so everyone would know -
or guess - he shrugged his pain aside; a cruel
pretence - ignoring only made it grow.

The gun was in his shirt. He felt it grow
in his imagination till the school
was scarcely big enough to hold it. 'Blow
them all away,' he muttered, 'watch this fool
show how I choose to let them live, or know
my fear, my agony. I can be cruel

as any of them, wicked, vile and cruel
enough to threaten, watch their terror grow,
eliminate them. Not bad for a fool.'
And he became a vast colossus, blow
by blow annihilating half the school
- it seemed - as trickling blood formed rivers. 'No,

Oh no!' he wailed and screamed and sobbed, 'Oh no!'
He'd only wanted them to stop, not cruel
revenge. He'd thought the gun would make them grow
to care, respect him. Too late now. The school
would not recover from this savage blow.
He knew he'd blundered, proved himself the fool.

But this was real. No fooling now. And no
forgiveness, just a growing pit, a cruel
revenge. And school would deal the final blow.

WELL WATER

More still than glass,
more dark than glass
well water waits
unfathomable.

Its chill
shivers spider webs,
tingles passages,
ghosts stone flags.

It is silent;
it skulks
drenching menace,
steeping dreams.

It gives us life,
gives us hope.
It purifies. It drowns.
Reflect.

TOTAL IMMERSION

Bare chests are concave; shorts flap
at broomhandle legs. Four boys call coarse
in school's-out-laughter, jostle,
each teasing others to the brink.

Gates trap river water in a dock,
its black inviting where sun tightens flesh.
Loose chains are no barrier
as boys nudge closer,
skittle the edge and topple.

One scrambles free, swings his legs,
fish-slithers out -
then dives back in, quicksilver.
The gathering crowd bites warnings to applaud.

Now all four describe a circuit,
water, dock and water, risking silt,
daring gravel with bare feet, squealing
each time iced shock catches breath.

They are heroes, their impromptu show
played to a gallery where adults grin
at gestures of success; and then
recalling reckless games, toss coins.

Rewards imply a grimmer sport.
The circle wheels faster, heaves and shoves,
earnest gasps replacing whoops.

This lesson teaches clamouring for cash,
out-ratting rivals from the race.
Classroom camaraderie is gone;
new studies isolate and swamp.

The crowd tires, disperses: no point now
in chancing cramp,
slimed drag of crannied walls. Four boys
let breezes dry their skin and tousle hair.

And there at the river's dock
childsplay is jettisoned: immersion total.

WATERSKIERS

Gemini figures, each holds a cord
behind their water-skimming mother,
stretches, arches into her curves.
Now close, now far apart, they form
intricate patterns, weave and swoop,
wet-suited swallows teasing summer
from leaden July.
They wave and call, words wind-whipped
as spun foam, each pass a loop
in their unbroken journey.

Look away, and they are gone.
Only twin wakes show
that they were here, breathed this air,
felt this water sprayed on skin.

Their boat, unladen now,
moves slowly back to berth.

LADY OF THE LAKE

Water locked, the lady thrusts her sword
to mark lake's centre, drawing
lord and knight. Unsheathed
the blade cuts diamond swathes in air,
each face a droplet snaring sun.

Rough seizing makes her fingers bleed
tracing rust paths down her palm, her wrist.
Her hand's closed curve
whorls under water's surface;
from its vortex
concentric ripples emanate
to lick the shore.

Her essence is imprinted: banks breathe,
rocks sweat her presence.
Here is power to cleanse, unstain, dissolve,
accomplish saltless sea change.

To this fixed pivot every woman comes
and hovers at lake's margin dipping toes,
or plunges soundless depths. Atoms
of water penetrate, drawn to the heart
by some osmosis learned pre-birth.

Lake's lady calls more clearly
than moon summoning brine's tide,
gives shroud or samite; offers chains,
lets her sisters use them
to subjugate the world or bind themselves;
while she remains, sustains,
floats,
anchors.

ENDEAVOUR - RESOLUTION - ADVENTURE - DISCOVERY
for Captain James Cook

How many nights adrift did he dream salt
in that ship timbered attic? Did the creak
of ropes that held his hammock echo sound
of breezes in the rigging? As he swung
did cobalt images invade his mind?
Reality of cold, the Yorkshire chill
of Marton, Ayton, Staithes and Whitby must
have frozen thought. Could he anticipate
exotic beaches, palm trees, tropic breeze?

How often was he woken by the light
of rising stars that filled high windows, shone
to jewel the night? In fantasy, perhaps,
each pane became a porthole, and each star
assumed new angles just as if his cot
was pitching while a wave swell rolled the ship.

By day, the mew of North Sea gulls became
translated into parrot's squawk, ape's call.
Landlocked in winter, did he pace the quay -
a stranded deck - and gaze beyond the point
where slate and pewter fused horizon's edge?

A solitary lad, instead of friends
his books were his companions - yielded thoughts
to dance in candle's flicker, speak to him.
Each page he turned, imagination drained
until words faded, and blank paper spread
its leaves, all resonant with space to fill
with charts and coastlines, islands never dreamed.

From birth, through childhood, youth, apprenticeship,

one burning drive forced his explorer's heart -
one mantra chanted in the throb of brine:
Endeavour, Resolution filled his soul -
Adventure - and at last, Discovery.

A MATTER OF SCALE

I stir the pool's glass,
watch hermit crabs no bigger
than my fingernail scuttle,
shell burdened, glittering
where sun dapples, drenched in brine.

What do they know of oceans,
vastness of Africa past the horizon,
wrecks and dolphins? What
do they need to know?

Their days are conflict,
battles to protect
territory of a shell, battles
to annexe another.

Insects skim the glass,
hardly stir its surface tension,
offer shade where tiny fish dart.

I look up beyond cloud shadow,
look around to note my boundaries,
compare inner space with breadth
that stretches further than imagining,

wonder who is reaching
to stir the glass of my pool.

A QUESTION OF DYING

Death was easy here,
trickling through undrained water,
nestling in breath -
scything babies, fit young men.

Bracing winter walks
iced lungs, crabbed sinews:
summer sun heightened
decomposition's stench.

Here mourning clothes
became familiar garments,
music was the measure
of a passing bell.

So why did God
pin down to life
his half-blind servant Patrick
for more than eighty years of pain,

to grieve Maria,
Maria and Elizabeth,
Branwell, Emily and Anne,
Charlotte and her unborn child?

CHARLOTTE BRONTE'S RING

Charlotte's room; instinctively
we whisper, fearing to disturb the ghost
whose walls absorb a thousand cries:
  'Wasn't she tiny!'
  'Fancy having a graveyard under your window!'
  'Look at the size of those shoes!'
And I am mesmerised, my gaze on gold
where tiny studs and loops
are chain-linked in a ring.

I exclaim not just to see its replica
among the tourist trappings, but to find
a perfect fit. Her ring belongs
on my finger, sits warm against my skin.

Outside, November drizzle oils fallen leaves.
I stumble on the cobbled path;
gold glints where I reach for the rough wall.
I drive away through Haworth mist,
risk narrow lanes -
a miniature beacon beams
where I grip the wheel.

Gold gleams from the hand
curled around my pen,
urges trails of ink on paper,
prompts poetry and stories, forges
a familiar groove in flesh.

VIRGIL'S TOMB: MERGELLINA

The journey starts in dusty afternoons
where rows of green frocked girls
declined and conjugated, sneaking answers,
attained the Aeneid with spots and bras,
sweated through O-levels, the sack of Troy.

For years the poet rested, shunted
into sidings cut from dusters,
walled in washing powder, emerging
only to surprise with crossword answers.

Now the route moves a stuffy train
through sun's blare, skims Naples heat
to rest in tree lined paths.
Beside the station stand
tombs for two poets;
Giacomo Leopardi's solid stone,
its massive cave gouged from the hill,
light flooded; and still higher,
beyond the aqueduct, a beehive of rock
cradles relics of Publius Virgilius Maro.

Breathless from slope and steps at noon,
I cannot speak - pace slowly round
the iron bowl - strange monument,
rusted, with laurel wreath and dry stalks
tied in faded pink ribbon. Outside
pigeons call, trains hiss, flowers
are musk heavy. Here
away from Trojan horse, from Dido's passion,
peace enfolds those bones
whose living essence cursed schooldays.

This is no place to linger, and all intents
to dance on your grave evaporate;
but as I go, I pick
two cracked, brown leaves from your poet's crown,
carry them home a thousand miles.

DOVE COTTAGE, GRASMERE

The guide admits us. I ease
my foot from its sandal,
let my bare sole slide flags
whose stone was warmed
by open fires - a Dove and Olive welcome.

Edging round the door jamb,
I imagine your shadow on the bed,
feel the moulded wood along my spine.

Did you rhyme the stream
that chills your larder? ...
speak sonnets as you planted
shrubs and herbs? ... pace
pentameters around your study?

Our guide talks cuckoo clocks and passports,
name-drops Coleridge, De Quincey.
I slip away to your writing room,
perch guilty in your chair
and lean against the rope.

Here I connect; for here the very air
is galvanised, breathes poetry.
I am Michael, I
your Solitary Reaper;
I stand on Westminster Bridge, above Tintern Abbey;
I celebrate your Daffodils and Butterfly.

Joining the others, I exclaim
at journals, gingerbread,
walls papered with The Times ...
content. In this place my thoughts
can fuse with yours, cross centuries
of lake and fell,
link in tumbling screes of words.

ALTERNATIVE REMEDY - DOVE COTTAGE

That small blue stone found in your dressing case
is veined with hope. Some ease from pain? a cure
to heal your troubled eyes? - what faith to place
in that blue stone found in your dressing case.
You held it tightly, pressed it to your face,
until it chafed and rubbed your eyelids sore.
That small blue stone found in your dressing case
is veined with hope ... some ease from pain ... a cure.

MURHILL HOUSE - SATURDAY AFTERNOON

The cheese and fruit are finished, and we go
from tidied kitchen through the afternoon
to find a place to write. The ebb and flow
of conversation stutters, stops. My room
of valley view and high, fine linened bed
is beckoning. I stretch out, close my eyes
to let imagination fill my head,
not distant trains, green slopes or cloudless skies.
I feel the rhythm of this magic day -
although I am awake, not rocked by sleep -
I feel the walls, joists, lintels gently sway,
hear murmured tones, both resonant and deep.
  This house reverberates its harmony
  in time with cataracts of poetry.

DREAM HOUSE

I dream my love a house
close meshed with wattle, sealed
with filigree of leaves. Here sunlight filters
patterns on the bed, the floor, on us
where we lie close, naked and silent.

I dream my love a house
strong in stone, safe walled,
grey and cool. It protects
when wind and storm threaten,
seals us within when strangers intrude.

I dream my love a house
loose with sticks, tight with stones,
washed with perfumes
of earth and air,
ever ours, impregnable.

MOTHER'S DAY PRESENT

not a manacle
not a duty gift
not a bribe
not a chain
not pregnant with subtext
not a protest
not an accusation
not guilty
not overstated
not a burden

but a bond
locking mother and daughters
throwing away the key

COMFORTER

In the car's warm womb she is curled,
sucking her thumb, rocked by motorway rhythms.
I carry her once again, counting
miles not months, half wanting
to thrust her free, and half
to hold her safe for ever.

November night is cold. We shiver
through first tinge of greying dawn,
reach the terminal; know our paths divide.

Passport. Tickets. She scrabbles in her bag,
proffers them, eager as the child
who made a card in school,
drew daffodils for Mothers' Day.

Five a.m. I mention coffee. She chooses
burgers, fries; licks mayo from her fingers,
giggles. I see honey sandwiches,
the crusts cut off, pulped,
sticky smeared on face and hair.

We waste our last minutes choosing books -
crosswords and a gossip magazine -
five minutes, twenty years
since join-the-dots and ABC.

Her flight is called. She hugs me, turns,
takes first steps on her journey around the world,
does not look back.

I make my way to the car,
make foetal curl behind the wheel;
try the taste of my thumb.

CONTACT

Ritual done, sterile as Pilate
the team of surgeons gathers,
cuts, excises, cleanses.

Bloodied gloves are binned.

Your hands, my father, are the lifeline
for liquids dripping in,
for pulsebeats measured out.

Practical hands; your gestures make
a mime of actions showing how they stripped
the pins that stitched your chest.
And I remember watching
your hands at plane and chisel,
your fingers threading my shoelaces.

And suddenly I do not know
how to hold your hand. A nurse
sits with me, her arm across my shoulders,
twines my fingers around yours
to catch their last warm moments.

Before I leave, pick up the life you gave me,
I wash my hands.

FOLLOWING NURSE'S INSTRUCTIONS
for Mum

Saturday afternoon: unfamiliar, this week
breaks routine, replaces shops
with standing by your narrow bed
as breathing ebbs. And I must strip
the rings from hands that cradled me.

I take three square-cut diamonds
on the band that bound
your wedding day to mine; the ring I wore
for 'something old' has blessed us both.

The others do not yield so easily. Flaccid fingers
mould around them. I have to edge
the next ring past your knuckle -
diamonds forever, fleeting their part
through your eternity.

I recall you laughing, explaining Grandma
picked your wedding ring - now finger fixed
for fifty years. Its joy dissolved
when you were widowed, dessicated
without your life's leaven.

I dribble liquid soap around the gold
whose rubies gleam four decades,
soothe it off; catch, too, sapphires,
the substitutes you chose when those Dad bought
were stolen. Their memories weigh more
than stone.

I remember how you gave up hope
the day they handed you his wedding ring.
Today your rings burn brands into my palm.
I slip their burden on my fingers,
assume your place - and feel the circle close.

FATHER

He left me with no directions
when he started his own uncharted journey.
I had to grope my route
through roads where houses stood
on one side only, and the other reached
amorphous tendrils into middle distance.

At first, saying 'Mum' was hard.
'And Dad' rolled easy in my tongue,
prickled behind my eyes. I had to stop
my mind from hoarding phrases
I must remember to tell him next time ...

Then one day, while I was still learning loss,
he came again to guide me,
mapped the maze of streets
he knew and I did not. His voice
steered words through my head, led me
back into familiar paths.

He has been silent since that day.
I feel myself edging further from him,
inching time and distance; yet now
I realise the worth of listening
on undiscovered wavelengths, know
new ways to communicate.

BIN BAGS

From boxes, plastic bags and biscuit tins
I gathered harvest of each birthday card,
each Christmas message, pressed flowers, cuttings, things
I never knew you kept. And it was hard
to throw your hoard away; but common sense
dictated that I must. I filled up nine
black rubbish sacks, and stacked them by the fence -
your lifetime's treasures waiting in a line
to join the other garbage on the tip.
I watched the trash collectors heave their load
to cram the truck's mouth, saw its wide jaws rip
then swallow as it crawled along the road.
A final wisp of dust hung in the air -
last relic of the life we used to share.

UNLOCKING DAD'S WORKSHOP

To come in here is hard. Sawdust,
the warm smell of oil, your radio recede.
Tools for your next task mock from the bench.

My husband takes your jacket from the door,
shrugs into it, learns
the shape and weight of file and saw and chisel.

Though tears distort, I see his smile,
incredible blue of eyes, deft fingers -
know why I chose him; know why
I can stop grieving you.

CHRISTMAS PRESENT

Slowly you cross the room to where I sit,
arms hugging knees, beside the fire.
You offer wine and whispers; candles flare
the grey-blue of your eyes. You mesh your fingers, mine
winding tinsel strands to bind us.

Faint strain of carols frosts outside. I trace
the contour of your cheek, jaw, neck,
press my hand flat on your heart
to feel the resonance of Christmases
all cinnamon and spice in memory.

We hold each other close: your skin's scent
makes me tremble. Tree and parcels fade,
the cards recede. Everything is you and I
forged one, compelled by charged caresses,
incandescent as the guiding star.

BRACELET

Its cold, boxed links
unwind to sense the curve of wrist,
learn flesh.

Gold whose temperature was constant
discovers warmth from skin,
knows the throb as blood beats.

Slipping back and forth
is already familiar, becomes
natural as touching.

Links mould to reflect
every shift of angle,
network pore and hair.

Consummation makes the arm
unaware of its chains;
makes chains forget the box.

GRACEFULLY?

Let us prove, my love, once more
we are not too old to break the rules:
that you can sneak into my room,
strip to smooth tanned skin,
slide into my bed.

Let us tell the world we're going for a stroll.
Then I shall peel away
day's trappings, let responsibility
slip down to my ankles.
I shall jigsaw into your arms.

Let us kiss till our lips ache,
touch and stroke
with first time urgency.
We won't mention aching backs, the weather;
we'll have no need of words.

And later, when we've unlocked the door,
I shall dress chaste in blue and silver,
smile small talk, scintillate politely.
And no one will guess we're not too old.

DÉJÀ VU

We don't do this any more,
painting, paper hanging;
don't climb ladders, fix borders -
but here we are, clinging to a picture rail,
spreading 'peach sunshine'
to span the space between us.

I wobble, nearly fall, and you laugh.
I touch one finger to the paint,
dab it on your nose ...
... and we are twenty again, letting light
spill down mushroom dark walls,
ooze along our fingers. You retaliate,
splashing my hair, my T shirt.
You hug me, hold the years back.

Our daughter arrives with tea,
mutters about painting the room
not each other, says something
about growing up.

PEARLS

Freed from their thread,
a waterfall of miniature moons
spills over my hand,
fills each dark crevice in the drawer;
no outfall, these,
from dragons fighting in the sky,
nor some oblation poured for Isis,
but most precious of my wedding gifts.

Now, even scattered in the dull of wood,
each crystal's axis catches light,
reflects, refracts soft rainbows. I collect
a handful, scoop them up,
pick through chains and scarves and boxes
to secure each globe.

Only when the string is drawn once more,
when eye and hand have fixed
their graduation, do I find
the grasp of pearls is tighter, and some beads
must have eluded searching fingers.
Solitary as in their oyster womb
they glimmer in corners, nacred with dust.

But errant pearls do not diminish;
they enhance the necklace,
clutch its promises,
concentrate its lustre.

I know again the first feel
of smooth rounds circling my neck,
glow of their creamy orient,
cool clasp of angels' tears a talisman
for luck and love.

NUDES, WITH ORANGE

Two oranges jostle the bowl
and I, naked and filled of you,
take the larger, touch its cool, rough skin
to your smooth flesh. I roll it,
staining your chest with its essence.

You do not speak; smile as I force my thumbs
to penetrate the peel, expose cream-threaded pith.
Zest droplets zing,
arc the air, spatter your face.
I tongue-tease them, taste juice.

Tempted, I split the globe
into two hemispheres, strip one segment.
I slide its tip through my teeth,
insinuate the rest between your lips,
and at the pivot of its symmetry
our kiss severs, bisects.

The pressure of your mouth on mine
makes orange trickle down my throat.
I run a coil of peel across your shoulder,
kiss your eyes, your cheeks, your neck,
exhale sun-flavoured breath
to scent firm contours of your body.

You take the fruit, crush me as you squeeze
last drops to lace my breasts,
suck spun gold till you have glutted.
Your heart slows, breathing evens.
I reach toward the bowl, and with one finger
caress the other orange.

JOHN DOE: D.O.A.

When the anger of metal subsides,
the Y has revealed its secrets,
last passes of scalpel shave
thin slivers from his fingers. Slowly,
tenderly they are eased onto living hands,
finding breath, pores and pulse.

His hidden self is disinterred
when fingerprints pronounce a name,
whisper a son, hint last address.
No longer only known to God,
he lives in driver's licence, union card,
breathes in phone listings.

Stripping off the loops of his signature,
signing forms to close another case,
the autopsy technician scrubs his hands:
cannot remove traces every contact leaves,
sees with his own eyes, but keeps
the dead man's touch alive.

MOVING ON

Don't weep a sea for me when I am dead.
Let all the happy memories fill your head,
reminding of the love we used to share.
Be certain that my spirit could not bear
your weight of mourning, pain of tears you shed.

If you can face that time with smiles instead
of tears, recall how many times we said
that death could never part us; don't despair,
  don't weep a sea for me.

My essence will remain, a figurehead,
a talisman to guard you in my stead.
Don't think that I could leave you. Everywhere
you go, my soul goes with you, always there.
Move on with joy and hope, not fear or dread.
  Don't weep a sea for me.

OVERSEAS POSTING

Listen while stones speak. Hear murmur
of the men who tramped through Gaul,
joined their garrison in lands
where apples ripened, vine and lemon
were unknown. Know their lament.

Feel wind that chilled their sweat
before it ran, and walk the sponge
of Welsh-weathered green
in place of lizard dust.

Sense excitement as they stirred
to pale girls with sapphire eyes,
and whored and wived away from home.
Imagine how language lilt rang smooth
on ears coarsened by Latin consonants.

Could you bear exile in the valleys?
Could you leave father, daughter,
feeling pressure of their last embrace
still moulding your torso? Could you
play rough in pool and palaestra, and drink
oblivion from amphorae of wine?
Could you keep faith with gods
who fated this on you?

From Pompei to Caerleon is now a day
of duty-free in Naples airport,
plastic-trayed boeuf bourgignonne,
case-carousel in Manchester, M6, M5.

But freeze frame a moment
to let whispers in the breeze
bear messages from stone
and roar their secrets.

GEOMETRY - WINDERMERE

White triangles shark water,
tacking a procession
beyond, against the wind. White birds
kite the sky.
Floating spheres skulk.
Cuboid jetties,
pinstriped with decking,
embrace the lake's edge.
A vast ellipse,
two dimensional and bottomless,
wrenches banks apart.

Among these ordered shapes, hints
of pi, Pythagoras, a mess of people
moves haphazard paths, jagged voices
fragmenting silence. They
sculpt body shapes
from air's mass, displace irregular channels,
disturb.

And yet their place is fixed; for they
locate the centre,
make volume from multiplication
side by side by side,
square the hypotenuse.

BUXTON RITUAL

The pattern never changed. One hovered
on double yellows while market crowds pressed,
the other queued in steam and grease,
and children ran between us
communicating 'lots of salt'
or 'breadcrumbs, not batter.' Then
the short drive downhill
- grey roads, grey houses -
to park where lake and trees
made an acute angle.

Ambrosia was whitest flakes of haddock,
vinegar and onions, gold slicked chips;
and grease marks on the new Dick Francis
never mattered. Hot and sated,
we stumbled from the car with scraps;
and ducks and geese, swans, pigeons
surged toward us.

Across the stream swings beckoned,
rides to make the day a party; blue
pool water enticed. At the Pavilion's core
we prowled gift shops, bought lemon cheese
or shoebags from the WI, chose ices.

Conservatory, Opera House, Victorian letter box -
we counted off each landmark
willing them to be there, fearing change.

Years away, I cannot remember
when the chain was broken - wonder
if I should have heeded warnings
in those ritual snapshots,

seen the woman gleam
in little girls' eyes. Perhaps the pool
still laps, the river flows,
they still serve chips in the market place.

These days we travel by a different route.

STAYING AT LEASOWE

Stark lines define a castle
where ordinary streets become
a swathe to cross the stray.
But this facade does not front
an echoing hall, old portraits.

We race the wind,
find warmth in Axminster,
follow the porter to our room
of mirrored wardrobes, TV,
a bathroom moulded in the turret's niche.

Cocktails and menus mellow evening
anticipating prawns and flambeed steak.
Alone but for the waiter, we touch hands
and feed each other strawberries.

Night is lush
with glimmer of street lamps,
white light from stars.
We lie awake
afraid of sleep dividing us.

Egg and bacon sizzle,
dissipate night's magic.
Spell released, we talk
about the Sunday market
and the tunnel home.

But Visa cards and cases can't dispel
impressions of a castle's romance,
a whispered swish of skirts,
ghost shimmer on the stair.

DAY TRIP TO HOLMFIRTH

These streets were made to be wet;
slopes and steps trap current
when rain starts at six
and never stops. We slosh
through car park, over bridge path,
find the dearest loos in Yorkshire.

Kerbs are laced by a frill of spray
where vehicles cram narrow roads.
A supermarket pulses life
at the town's centre, ordinary
as bread: and yet
a tipsy surrealism beckons.

An outsize garden gnome,
wellied and rough-trousered,
grins his welcome. Trippers snap
Sid's Cafe, pose on pavements, laugh
at the sign of The Wrinkled Stocking.

We dodge the deluge, find strong tea
and home made truffle cakes
above a treasure store of curios -
don't move; keep hands in pockets;
know we are under surveillance.

Gift shops lean, fairground crazy cottages,
all steps and corners. Their staff conspire
to keep a parallel universe alive,
acknowledge for the hundredth time
that Norah Batty dropped in earlier;
laugh as though the thought's original.

We lose an hour browsing,
and the bookshop shuts around us.
Wading back where grass and shrubs
have displaced gravestones,
we look for furtive lovers,
listen for footfalls where old soldiers stalk.

A mile on, rain stops.
We glance back, but hills have rolled
around the theme park of a town;
and Yorkshire's Brigadoon has gone, invisible
until next Sunday teatime.

STREET STATUES, BARCELONA

They never move until a tourist stands
before them posing for a snap, commands
this posture or those gestures; then they flow
in fluid motion, drifting to and fro
like liquid puppets moved by unseen hands.

The heat is unremitting. Work demands
bronze, gold or silver makeup. Hot sun brands
their bodies, scorches through metallic glow.
    They never move.

Each statue is an actor, understands
that suffering is art whose height withstands
all ordinary pain. They cannot go
until the final gasps at their tableaux
have faded into dusk, blown in the sands.
    They never move.

CIRCUMVESUVIANA

Sorrento: trains snooze, mouths open.
One, a silver snake, wakes up,
snaps shut its jaws, judders and slides.

Sant' Agnello: orange and lemon groves,
walnuts, olives flare
as windows frame their passing.

Castellamare: the train squints down
at half completed hulls of ships,
up where cable cars hiss on wires.

Pompeii Scavi: terracotta rusts the station,
points a new angle on Vesuvius.
Lines stretch back to Pliny.

Torre Annunziata: a blue shirted guard,
bored, chews gum; stamps crescent moons
in tickets.

Leopardi: sleeping cats are stretched in full sun
ignoring rumbles and whines as the train arrives,
whistles signalling departure.

Ercolano: the slow, insistent arc of track
hums. Hoardings are defaced,
new messages sprayed along the platform.

Portici - Bellavista: a brown rat
skitters over rails, through chippings,
claims a half sandwich.

Napoli: end of the line. Passengers
are disgorged, carriages swept:
and moving on rewinds the bay's curve.

BLUE GROTTO, CAPRI

Sea purges. Stain of sin is washed
from thighs before the couple's breathing slows.
Aquamarine thrust and lap
reflect on cavern walls.
Water warm as wine is an amniotic caress.

They swim, swing limbs onto a rock.
Applause. Laughter. The next pair dive
for their drenched consummation.
Watchers in the boat give hands and mouths.

Decadent echoes whisper still when worshippers
bring prayer and offerings to sea nymphs,
turn the pleasure cave into a shrine.

At Neptune's whim or Vulcan's
the island heaves in bradyseismic shock,
seals the grotto's entrance so tight
sun fingers cannot probe, and azure dims to indigo.

Dark powers usurp. The cave is coven
only dared by elementals.
Coral rusts the waterline, bloods the tide's edge.

As myth and mystery uncurl,
unknowing fear forms monsters.
Giant squid send tentacles
to coil the sleeping mind, swamp nightmares.

New generations shun the shadowed legend
hazard limestone arch
see again sunned shafts turn lapis lazuli;
define a trail for tourists.

Morning visitors lie flat against the rowing boat's base,
shiver in clammy dank,
exclaim at new colours, turquoise light or blue.
Their words reverberate until rock walls absorb them.

Patterns forged from water, earth and air
plot new dimensions,
know men are transient; things last.

Most constant is the sea -
uncreated - undestroyed -
its molecules enclosing time,
welding yesterday, today, tomorrow;
purging.

THE DEVIL'S PLOT - FUERTEVENTURA

A task for God: Franciscan brothers toiled
to build a monastery, the first to rise
beneath the bright Canaries sun, just north
of Betancuria. In dust and heat
the very rock pulsed with the devil's heart.

And he, the devil, was bewitched and forced
to carry boulders to the holy site.
Imagine how his anger must have seethed,
frustration blazing in his evil breast,
his cunning honed to plot for his escape.

At last his task was almost finished, but
he knew his captors had no mind to grant
him freedom. He must search for someone who
could be persuaded that the work was done,
could be persuaded he should be released.

He found a fool who would believe his word,
who let him go to roam the valley, climb
surrounding hills for seven hundred years.
Secure beside St. Bonaventure's church
he watched the generations rise and fall.

Today the ruins of the monastery
are part of landscape's magic; but don't go
too close - for in the well the devil sleeps
by day, crawls out at dusk, and through the night
he wanders freely on the mountainside.

PLOT A3: TARAJALEJO

'Imagine it with doors,' she said,
and standing in the shell
of her nearly-living-room
I knew partitions.

My daughter mimed
where chairs, fridge, beds would fit,
exaggerated stepping the threshold,
made hands a frame
to access views of garden, palm trees, cliffs.

I picked up a discarded tile,
held its smooth peach-and-stone
against my cheek, admired
its fellows jigsawed round the shower.

Together we clambered
over rubble, plumbed the pool's foundation,
laughed light as tropic sun
glittering through doorholes, window spaces.

'Imagine it with her,' I said,
weeks later, showing my husband
where our love was rooting.

But doors were fixed,
windows cold with dust-toughened glass,
and though we picked our way
through the nearly-garden,
walls kept us outside.

THROUGH A LENS, DARKLY

It will play on, my daughter, on and on -
that loop behind your eyes that reels the hours;
but nobody can change the ending. Time
rewinds. A celebration, travel reps
relaxing in the sunshine, and your friend
confides this is the best day of her life.
You have to call the office. You'll catch up.

And now you're driving to the meeting point,
the last stop, and ahead is chaos. Pause.
Freeze frame. There's blood on sand; the other reps
all hurled to lie with her sprawl by the jeep
that's toppled, wheels in air. You leave your car,
fast forward, knowing you can help. You kneel
to cradle her, stay with her on the route
she takes alone, two thousand miles from those
who eased her life's first journey into light.

Freeze frame. She ebbs, while all around the surge
of forcing life crescendoes. You can see
abortive fights to help the others, stem
with breath the essence spewing out, console
the inconsolable. Advance the film.
She cools within your arms despite the glare
of unrelenting sun. If you let go,
she's gone. Stills bring your thoughts in focus, fix
the caterers who think you can't be far;
my phone call draws you; two hotels whose guests
have no-one to complain to now. Freeze frame.

Now forward it past counsellors, past help,
to stop the week two funerals were filled
with grieving twenty-somethings. And move on
to laughter on the flight, to extra work
rescheduling their duties, training staff.

My daughter, we have both seen death close by,
both learned necessity of sharp relief,
of moving from its shadow into light.
We recognise the mist behind the lens.
The loop begins again. It will play on,
my daughter. Let it reel around your heart.